A Woman's Mind

By

Carla Horton

This book is a work of fiction. Places, events, and situations in this story are purely fictional. Any resemblance to actual persons, living or dead, is coincidental.

ISBN: 1-4033-9903-4 (e-book)
ISBN: 1-4033-9904-2 (Paperback)

Library of Congress Control Number: 2003091742

This book is printed on acid free paper.

Printed in the United States of America
Bloomington, IN

Photo: Comstock.com

1stBooks - rev. 03/13/03

Illustrations by my son,
Jullian M. Wilson

Dedication

I dedicated my book of poetry to my two boys,

Jullian Michael

and

Jeremy Austin (may you rest in peace)

Mommy loves you'll.

About The Book

"A Woman's Mind", is a book of poetry of my thoughts and experiences that span 20 years ...about what some of us, if not all, as women feel, think and go through, in dealing with relationships. How we cope in different situations...while maintaining our self esteem.

TABLE OF CONTENTS

A LETTER TO JEREMY

Life still goes on…and on. People are laughing and crying, all for different reasons…but you're not here. You're resting peaceful now, from this hard world…how's it going up there? I know that everything's fine…you're laughing and playing…no more tears, no more fears, no more pain. I thank God for that…but I still miss you…painfully. I know as time passes the emptiness will become less …as I recall all of the wonderful memories. I just want to thank you again for fighting for thirteen long years…so that I was able to be your mother…I count it a privilege. Everyone says, "hi" and sends their love, along with their hugs and kisses. We love you Jeremy "Pooh Bears" and we will always miss you and your beautiful smile.

Love always,
Mommy

PART ONE: A WOMAN'S MIND

Carla Horton

A WOMAN'S MIND

A womans mind is like a memory bank.
No matter what the information is, she'll
be able to recall it, even those she wishes
to forget.
My advice to husbands and lovers, is to
make sure she see's and hear's the positive
words and actions, more than the negative.
(basically making sure positive out weighs
negative).
That is, of course, if you really love her and
want her in your life forever.

TALK TO ME

Talk to me. Massage my mind with your
words of wisdom and knowledge, dreams and
fantasies.
Talk to me, if you want to get to know me.
Don't give me lines of lies. Just give me
honesty and realness.

Carla Horton

STRENGTH

Does my pain cause you happiness?
Does it make you feel strong, superior,
or bring you joy?
What do you gain from putting me
down?
Is it that you're trying to break me in
some way?

Do you think that my strength comes from
you?
Well, I'm here to tell you that, OH NO
BUDDY IT DOESN'T!" MY STRENGTH
COMES FROM THE LORD!!!
SO THE MORE YOU TRY TO BREAK ME,
THE STRONGER I GET!

Carla Horton

LONELINESS

Loneliness comes in all kind of ways.
In a crowd of people, married or single,
rich or poor.
If you have children, they will keep you
busy. They'll give you their hugs and
kisses, especially if they think you
look a little down. That lifts you
up in a different way. In a parental
blessed way.

When you are married and need that
special hug from your husband. That
hug that let's you know that everything
will be okay because you have each other,
but, all you get is a frown or a blank stare
like, "what"? That is just about the
loneliest time.
So we say to ourselves, "that's okay, I
will be alright", and then we go on
about our business and make another
day.

GEM

I am a gem…a unique individual.
A very, very, precious and special
lady. I know and love this about
myself. I refuse to be treated less than
such.

Carla Horton

KNOW YOURSELF

I kiss myself. I reward myself.
One must love themselves before
they can love another.
Know yourself…your wants, needs,
and desires. Know them inside out, so
when you began to love another,
you will not loose you. You will
have your own unique self to offer.

THE TELEPHONE

Ring, Ring, Ring
The telephone echo's a
familiar sound. Which usually
means that there is someone on
the other end, confirming, making
plans, cancelling plans, talking sweet
nothings, ending or beginning romance.

The list could go on and on. Some
people understand this system, others
it seems too confusing, complicated
or they just can't catch the rhythm of
…using the telephone.

BEING THERE

Why can't you be there for me, just like
I'm there for you? Put the machismo aside
and be yourself. I promise that I will try
not to hurt you, all I want to do is love
you. The only thing I ask, is that, promise
you'll be there for me, like I'm there for
you.

Carla Horton

MAKE IT

We can make it through anything…anything, because
we're together as one.
Just please don't put your hands on me, to hit me nor
to throw me, because then that just closed the door
on the union…relationship and made us two.
Now, I'm going my way and please go yours.

MY VOICE

Who's been whispering sweet nothings in your ear?
Expressing their love and desire for you. Oh please
don't say nobody. Don't insult me that way. I
would know that it was a lie. I mean come on now.
For years you were in love with me and my voice
from good morning until goodnight.

You said
it sounded so soft, sweet, beautiful and sometimes
like a melody.
But now, you say that you can't stand to hear my
voice.
So I ask you again…who's been whispering sweet
nothings in your ear, expressing their love for you
or desire to be with you?

TRUE LOVE...UNCONDITIONALLY

I refuse to believe that true love, unconditionally,
along with romance and a lifetime of happiness does
not exist.
I refuse to believe that the same man that professes
his love for you and thinks that you are the sunshine
of his life and the beat in his heart, can't still love
you the same way once you're married.
I have yet to find that man, but just as sure as I
know that there is a GOD in heaven, a good
man like that does exist.

Carla Horton

LOVE ALL OF ME

I wish there was someone to love my wild,
crazy, zany ways…as well as my together,
cool, nothing every bothers me facade.
Appreciate my serious, courageous side, and
not just want me for my eccentric, erotic and exotic
mind.

LOVE...A LEGAL DRUG

Love is like a legal drug.
Once you open your heart to
actually feel love, you're hooked.
It compasses you totally. It's a feeling
unlike any other...

it's an extraordinary emotion.
It's very amazing how that same love that
feels so good, can also hurt when the heart
is broken.

WASTE OF TIME?

Is it a waste of time when a relationship ends,
the bond breaks and love is no more
…or is it an
experience and you try not to go the same route
again…although that's what you said last time.
Of course this was different…different love,
different meaning, different situations…but the
same pain in the end.

Carla Horton

TEARS

Tears flow so fluently now.
Suddenly my eyes tear up, sting and then
tears stream down before I have a chance
to realize what's happened. Oh there isn't
a need to analyze what's happening. The
pain that lies deep within, hidden behind a
beautiful smile…

has decided to detour around
the obvious path, where I may actually be able
to push it back down and has reached the surface
through another door… allowing me and my
system to wash clean of the hurt and pain
and become refreshed again.

Carla Horton

WHAT TO DO

I started drawing today... nothing in particular...just
lines. First they were straight, then they started
curving and curving and curving until it looked
like a big ball of inked yarn.
I couldn't lead the pen away from the ball, because
it was exactly how I was feeling inside...sad,
confused, hurt, scared...not knowing what to
do...what changes to make in my life...

am I to sit and wait, or to go straight ahead....dive
right in, but holding tightly to the reins...not
go too fast too soon, knowing the demands of being
a single mom of a teenager and the mom of a special
needs child.
Yet, I have the need to exercise my mind, mingle and
oh yeah...pay the bills without feeling strapped.

Lord, I need a clear answer on what to do, but in
the meantime, I'll wait on you and continue to
sing praises to your name. Amen

Carla Horton

CHOCOLATE/CREAM

Do you see me? Do you feel the sweet tension that
seems to flow between us whenever we are in the
same room?
Although the words are not spoken, our body language
move in the same rhythm. Our eyes connect to each
others so strong. I wonder if the hesitation is because
we have two different backgrounds...

I mean…me being
chocolate and you being cream.
This situation is not new to me, but I wonder if this
would be new to you.
Only time will tell…if we are suppose to get to a
higher
level…if so,
I know it will happen. I don't want just a fling,
I want something a whole lot deeper.

Carla Horton

THINKING

I'm sitting out here on my porch…thinking
about the end of summer drawing nigh…
with the beginning of fall coming near.
School will begin again…the holidays
are around the corner…then begins a New Year.

Carla Horton

The cold will cease…the snow will melt…
spring will come…school's out…summer arrives,
and where am I? Sitting out here on the porch…
thinking about the end of summer drawing nigh…
another year has just passed by…what have I
accomplished?

MIND GAMES

Mind games…word games…mindless wordings
coupling into sentences with no meaning…no root…
just dangling free in the air from your mouth…all
feels the same…like you're playing games…with me-
perhaps…
but actually with yourself.

You see…or what you don't
see is that I'm not in your game, because I recognize what's
going on…I see your game. I'm just amusing myself to see
when you will tire out and become real…leaving the
childish playground behind.

FREE FALLING

Enhancing…embracing…embarking on a love
that should be, could be and one day maybe…
but you seemed to have dropped the ball…
leaving my love free falling into thin air…

Carla Horton

free from your grasp, that was once held so
dear in the palm of your hand... until you got
careless and it has left you behind...all by itself
again...until one day, trusting another not to drop the
love... that is genuinely given.

TAKE SOMETHING FROM TODAY

The days that pass are not actually gone…
that is if you learned something from them.
It could be just a word spoken…a deed
that was done to enhance your life…
someone else's life…
your thought process…

making you to think about things a little
differently.
No matter if the day went fast or slow, take
something from it, so it wouldn't have been
wasted…because you can't live in the past.

KEEPING LOVE REAL

Magic is being able to make illusions seem like reality. It's all in good fun…entertaining. Some people treat love like that. Oh it is definitely a scarey thought, but true.

Let's keep love real…honest… and open to all the wonderful adventures that it offers a man and a woman.

Carla Horton

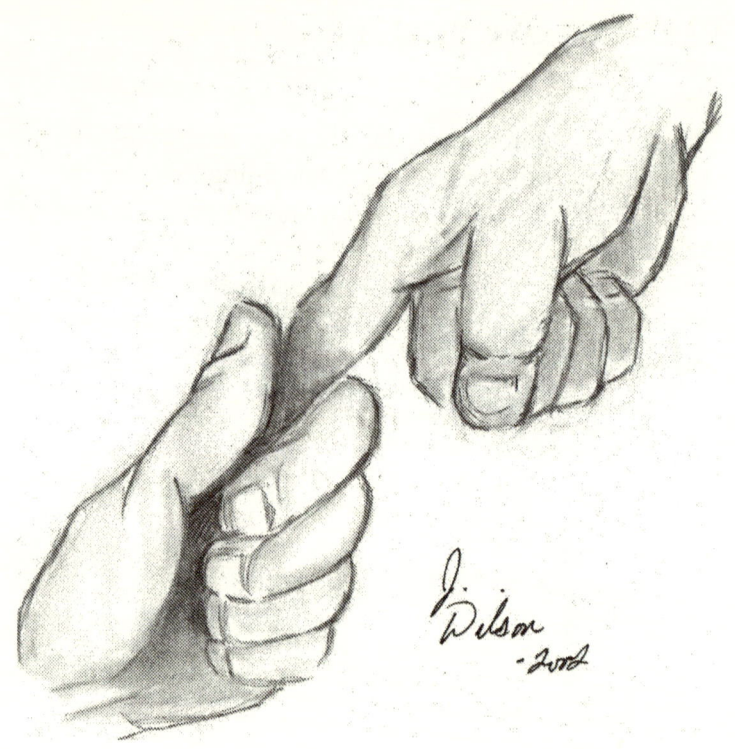

CALL MEN...MEN

Don't call men dogs. Why not?...
because not all men helped coin the phrase.
There are good men around...
and the men whose behaviors are questionable...
we let them off the hook of having
to take responsibility for their actions...it
allows them to behave irresponsibly...

no… call men what they are…MEN.
Now they must handle or fix a situation they
caused like a man should…and then the young
men coming after them will watch and do the same.

YOUR LOVE

Your love allows me to feel like a woman.
Your love makes me feel protected.
Your love allows me to feel that…
it's okay to show my vulnerable side
and still remain strong.

Your love makes me want to cry…
not because I'm sad…but
because I feel that I finally know how
it feels to be loved by a man…
my man…unconditionally.

Carla Horton

OCEAN LOVE

The waves of the ocean...over lapping each other...
moving into one another...up and down...together...
rolling over and over in harmony...
like lovers entangled
in each other...moving together in pure ecstasy...
calming
down...only after the tidal wave rises to it's peak,
releasing the love...
joining us together as one.

PART 2

A WOMAN'S MIND-EMOTIONS

Carla Horton

I CRY BECAUSE…

I cry not because I miss the person…I cry
because I miss the relationship…union…
togetherness of being one…the bond…
closeness…unity and inner sanctum that
two people in love…have…share…create…
are…become

EMOTIONAL VULNERABILITY

A lot of people get caught up in
emotional vulnerability…

that's when a person reacts to the way
a person hurt them… by compounding
the hurt and racing to another for comfort…

instead of…
soul searching and thinking of how
to go on and heal from the pain…
re-examining themselves… and
finding themselves…all over again.

JUST FRIENDS?

Would it be much simpler for me to just
see and think of you as
"just a friend"?
Just someone to hang out with every now and then.
Having conversations on the telephone…ol' buddy ol'
pal.
Nothing too deep or meaningful on an
intimate…personal level…
just a "hey, what's up".

Could that actually happen?
I mean, can I actually disconnect my emotions
and stop feeling for you the way I do?
It seems to me as if you could with no problem.
The main question that I ask myself is…
do I really want to disconnect?
No not really… but acting as if I could,
helps to keep my feelings in checked…
helps to quiet the emotional drama going on inside.

Carla Horton

ROMANCE ME

I may be crying now...I may be wondering
what happened to the love we could of had...
should of had....but it takes two to be in love,
and I'm tired of being in it all by myself.
I deserve better. I want more from you...
slow dancing...candlelight dinners...
holding hands...walking arm in arm...

being surprised by you...
just because you love me
and want to see me happy...
be happy... by you...
because the affection of love is
being shown through you...
from you...to me.

Carla Horton

CAMOUFLAGED LOVE

The depth of my love for you, flows as wide
as it does deep...but, it is camouflaged as your
"special friend" although...that phrase within itself
describes us too.
We share on many different levels...
none which can be described,
because to do so, would seem to
dilute what we share.

NEW LOVE

Why is it that when we have that
new "special" love in our life,
we have renewed energy.
It's as if we could run for days without stopping
and please…sleep…what's that?
but…when we get hurt and loves no more…
your heart has a hole in it…

sleep becomes your friend...as well as loneliness... until...love finds you once again. I have a better idea....just become your own best friend... even after you find...another new love.

WHO ARE YOU?

Who are you? I know who you say you are…
but who are you really?
I can see that you are a man.
I want to know the real you…
or do you know who you really are?
OH MY!…
have you gotten so caught up
in your own lies and games that you've
lost who you are?…

and when you look in the mirror,
do you not recognize the person staring back?
I have a suggestion...spend some quiet time by yourself...
and get to know YOU all over again...
before you dare approach another woman...
and definitely before approaching me again.

SEE...ME

Where do you go when you look at me?
Do you really see me or some form of me...
maybe your fantasy me...the spring flower...
so delicate swaying in the gentle breeze...
or maybe you see the business me...
making decisions on my own...
conquering fears and frustrations that
come along in my life...

and that happens to make you feel
a little uneasy… because I'm
doing it with the help of the Lord…
and on my own…and you feel there's no room for you.
How about seeing me…the real me…
the whole person…the delicate flower,
the business woman, the mother,
the lover, the friend …me.

HOPE...TRUE LOVE?

My friend thought she fell in love today,
but it turned out to be a farce.
A couple of months went by
and she knew for sure this new love
was the real deal,
but it turned out to be another farce,
just wearing a different face.
My friend thought she fell in love again today...
what?...did you think she had given up?...

no, no, no,
she cried, cursed, swore off looking for another love…
but days go by, tears dry up, hope comes alive and…
my friend thinks she fell in love today…
who's my friend?…
women everywhere who hope to find true love…
but girlfriend… take your time,
don't worry… true love will come your way.

AN EXTRA

You, me…she? You, me and…she?
Why do I feel that there is someone else in
our relationship?
Could it be the way you look at me now…
it has changed lately…not as loving, and soft,
but with criticism.

Carla Horton

Could it be the way you talk to me now
has become rare and harsh…
or could it be the way you dress and the cologne
you now wear has suddenly changed.
You, me, no…let me help you out…you and she.
I'll go find my own duet.

Carla Horton

IS THERE ROOM?

Open your door just a little wider... please...
I just want to get closer to that place you hold so
dear...
your heart.
I want to know is there room enough for me...
my love...for you...in there...
I promise to handle my precious space,
with special...special care...thank you.

CHEMISTRY

The chemistry that flows through us…
feels like an electric current…
charging through our bodies…
making me want you…with excitement…

and anticipation…of our bodies…
connecting…coming together as one…
loving every inch of each other…until completion…
and longing for more…

OPEN YOUR EYES

Open your eyes to see them,
before they see you.
they studied you…
before they approached…
and before you knew what was happening…
they already knew how they were going
to play the game.

Look around more intently…
gaze into the eyes staring
back at you…what do you see?
okay, now act accordingly…
with caution…

Carla Horton

THE SECRET CODE

There seems to be a secret code,
that men have today…when women
come their way.
It seems to be…stake out…meet…talk….
smile…act interested…
draw her in…just a little closer…
ah yes…she's interested…
now…

become aloof…disinterested…
commitment phobic…walk away from
what I started…becoming too real…
now on to the next one.

CAN I GET TO KNOW YOU?

knock...knock...um...yes...ah...
here's a lady that would like to get to
know you, if it's at all possible...
you do have a real side, don't you?

I mean a side that has real emotions…
not the cool public you…
but the behind the door emotional you…
the you that knows how to
connect on a more personable level.

ACTIONS AND REACTIONS

We are responsible for our own actions and
reactions…
you can't make another person be what you want…
either they are or are not what you're
looking for.

Carla Horton

You can not make another person…
love you…
even if they say they do,
but their actions say differently.
How you react to their actions is up to
you. You are only responsible for your own
actions and reactions.

GETTING OUT OF THE GAME

I'm wondering to myself…
while I'm crying on my bed….
if I should get out of this
love game,
before I start associating love with pain.
I'm the type that wants to be happy in love…
of course I know that love has it's rough days…

but lately it seems, as if…people want quantity love…
instead of quality love…
and the real love that the person feels for another…
becomes diluted and tainted.
People should learn to love one at a time
and give it all they've got…
and never allow someone else to enter…
because the innocent get hurt.

TOO MUCH ABSENCE

You say that absence makes the heart
grow fonder...
yes, I agree...to a certain degree...
but...too much absence makes a girl wonder...
does he miss me...really...as much as I miss him?...

Carla Horton

or is this just part of the game of love…
just a different version…like hide and seek.
If it's anything but real…
I choose to opt out,
so the man that wants real love can come.

WORTH HAVING

Nothing worth having comes easy…
so the saying goes…but in relationships,
it is a little easier if both parties are committed
to making it work…expressing their love, dreams
and desires for the relationship… for each other…

yes…everyone should have…
and must have their own interest in life…
but, when you're in a relationship…
the other person should also have top priority.

NEVER ALONE

As I'm sitting in my bed…alone and crying…
longing for you to come hold me…
because I need for the cares of the world,
to just float away…
while being held in your arms,
as we talk the night away…but…

while I was longing for you,
the Lord reminded me that I am not alone,
and that He would hold me close.
He also let me know,
as He's done so many times before,
that everything will be alright,
as he held me tight,
and that I will have a peaceful and restful night.
Thank you Lord Jesus, thank you.

SAVE YOUR TEARS

Girlfriend, save your tears,
even though your heart aches.
Yes, you're lonely and wishing for someone to love…
but love yourself, don't let yourself down.

Carla Horton

Count on God and yourself…
to get you through another day.
When you least expect it,
love will find it's way to you,
looking tall and handsome…
with a genuine smile… grinning from ear to ear.

ANTICIPATION

It has been such a very, very long time,
since I have anticipated a first kiss...
wondering when...where...how...
okay, maybe not how...but come on,
take your mind back...

yes you remember...how sweet
it was...and how sweet it will be...when
it happens again.
I am so happy that I can still find a kiss
so special and meaningful...soulful.

Carla Horton

BAGGAGE

As we get older, we seem to gather baggage.
Everyone has some kind of baggage. Some may be
light,
some heavy…close to calling it a mess or chaos…but,
it is all
in the way we handle our baggage.
Some of us have our baggage under control.
Some let their baggage control them, causing them
to trip and fall,
never getting a handle on their baggage,
affecting every area of their
life…
eventually, spinning them out of control.

SILLY ME...PART 1

I let my emotions get involved with my
head and heart...instead of thinking,
matter-of-fact,
I begin to think and feel a little deeper,
and now I'm holding my head in my hands
and wiping the tears from my eyes.
My heart aches now...
all because I begin to feel on a more intimate level.
I'm the only one to blame,
he most definitely made sure not to get close...
but saying, "come here ...I want to be with you",
at the same time...
"I'm not ready for a relationship...but let's hang out"
Excuse me...I can hang out with my girlfriends...
or someone else less confused.

Carla Horton

SILLY ME...PART 2

Hey, I guess I haven't gotten it down pat yet...
not to feel anything for someone...
but, my problem is...
when I allow a man to call me,
I'm saying let's see what "this" is about...
let's see if there is or could be a connection...
or not... but I never
thought, that two people would not
even get out of the starting gate... we're
still sitting in the nose bleed seats
watching life as it goes by...
instead of experiencing it together.

THE JOURNEY

The journey begins when one door closes
and another one opens. It is a new stage in life.
When the journey begins, do you travel it alone…
although with GOD, we are never alone,
but do we make the journey by ourselves
or share the journey with that special someone.

Would they even understand what you are
experiencing…
would they even care?
Would they love you enough and have faith enough to
help you see it through
or will they fizzle out at the start,
or during a crucial time like in the middle.
Some won't get a clue, until it is their time
and they hope you give them better…
than what they gave you.

The next two poems are definitely intended for the mature readers only.

Thank you.

Carla Horton

VIRTUAL REALITY

You have me living and moving in virtual reality…
my mind keeps reliving…
our sensual conversations of ecstasy and pleasures…
pleasing each others needs and fantasies…
anticipating us joining together and becoming one…
our bodies moving and touching…
swaying in rhythms…
and motions of pure excitement…
awakening every nerve in our bodies as we…
ah yes…and lay quietly…
gasping for air and anticipating…
talking about it all over again.

BURNING DESIRE

I have this burning desire to feel your body
against me…inside me
I have this burning desire to feel your hands
touching me…all over…inside me
I have this burning desire to feel your tongue
all over my body…inside me
I have this burning desire to feel you inside me
…making love to me

Carla Horton

MY FREE SPIRIT

In order for you to love me…
you have to understand…
me…
don't try to quiet the…
free spirit…
that God has blessed
inside of me.

About the Author

Carla Horton, is the mother of two boys, Jullian and Jeremy. Jullian is in college and Jeremy passed December 22, 2001.

Carla started writing poetry as a child. A poem called "Is There", that she wrote at the age of 12, was published in the children's magazine Jack and Jill. In 2000, she had another poem published in the International Library of Poetry book, "From Silver Fountains", called "I Cry Because"… and now she has published her first book of poetry titled "A Woman's Mind".